Alexander Graham Bell Invents the Telephone

❦

Young Alexander Graham Bell had devised a machine that carried the human voice up to twenty miles! But people laughed at him and called his telephone an electrical toy. What use would it be? So Bell traveled around giving demonstrations— even to Queen Victoria of England. Then people flocked to buy telephones—and poles and wires went up across America.

This is the amazing story of a single man's accomplishment, which began the era of modern communications.

Alexander Graham Bell Invents the Telephone

❧❧❧

FORMERLY CALLED

Mr. Bell Invents the Telephone

❧❧❧

BY KATHERINE B. SHIPPEN

RANDOM HOUSE · NEW YORK

Library of Congress Cataloging in Publication Data:
Shippen, Katherine Binney, 1892–1980
Alexander Graham Bell invents the telephone.
(Landmark books; 12).
Previously published as:
Mr. Bell invents the telephone.
1. Bell, Alexander Graham, 1847–1922.
2. Inventors—United States—Biography. I. Title.
[TK140.B37S5 1982] 621.385'092'4 [B] 82-284
ISBN: 0-394-85338-5 (pbk.); 0-394-95338-X (lib. bdg.) AACR2

The etching of Alexander Graham Bell that appears on chapter openings is
reprinted by permission of The Bettmann Archive. It shows Bell opening
the telephone line between New York and Chicago in 1892.

Manufactured in the United States of America
1 2 3 4 5 6 7 8 9 0

Contents

Acknowledgments

❧❦❧

The author wishes to make grateful acknowledgment to Ralph E. Mooney of the American Telephone & Telegraph Company for his assistance in gathering material for this book; and to Edward Hale Bierstadt for permission to use material from Catherine Mackenzie's book *Alexander Graham Bell, The Man Who Contracted Space*.

The following publishers have given generous permission to use quoted material:

Houghton Mifflin Company for three passages from *Alexander Graham Bell;*

The New York *Herald Tribune* for a passage from the New York *Tribune*, October 1876.

Alexander Graham Bell Invents the Telephone

1
A Young Man
Comes to Boston

"Boston! Boston!" The conductor's voice rang through the crowded railroad car. The locomotive came to a rattling stop with a snort of steam and a grating of the brakes against the wheels. The passengers took up their bags and began to climb down to the platform. The journey from Ontario, Canada, had been a long one. They were glad it was over. It was the first week in April 1871.

Alexander Graham Bell, then twenty-four years old, walked out with the crowd, through the door of the steam-filled, noisy station, into the street. The spring air was fresh with the smell of the sea. He paused for a moment to look up at a street sign, then turned to the left. He had never been in Boston before, but he had studied the map; he knew the way.

He walked quickly, carrying a small, leather-covered bag. People jostled against him on the narrow sidewalk; drays with straining horses splashed mud from the puddles in the street; horsecars rattled past. But Aleck, his hat pulled well down and the ends of his plaid muffler firmly tied beneath his chin, paid no attention. He was intent on his own thoughts.

He was well again now—that was the fact that was uppermost in his mind. The doctor back in London, where he had lived until a year ago, had said he might not live six months. Both of his brothers had died of tuberculosis, and Aleck himself had shown signs of the disease. So Aleck's father had immediately dropped his work as an elocution teacher, and his mother had packed up their things and sold their house in London. They had brought him to Canada, where he had rested for a year.

"Now I am well again," he said to himself as he hurried past a row of brick houses where maids with scrubbing brushes and buckets of soapy water were scouring the flights of steps. "Now I can work and earn my own living like anyone else. I'm starting a new life."

The new life that Aleck was starting that morning was the life of a teacher of the deaf. His father had followed the same profession and had made a great success with his system of "visible speech" in England and Canada. Now Aleck was to introduce that system into the United States.

In his breast pocket as he walked along was a letter from Miss Sarah Fuller, principal of the Boston School for the Deaf at 11 Pemberton Square. It offered him a position as lecturer. He put up his hand and felt the letter a little stiff against the rough wool of his coat.

"I never thought I'd be a teacher—not in the wide world," he mused. He had never liked school very much. "Once I thought I'd be a musician. Signor Bertolini believed I had talent—he said so. But then, after Signor Bertolini died, I lost interest in music somehow. And then I thought I'd give Shakespearean recitals—but that was only because my grandfather did it so well, and I wanted to imitate him. Somehow or other I seemed to forget about that too. And then this chance came—I wonder what it will be like at Miss Sarah Fuller's school."

He was glad, after all, that he was to be a teacher. It would be a wonderful thing to teach deaf children to speak. And Miss Fuller also wanted him to lecture to teachers of the deaf so that his influence would spread to many places outside Boston.

Yet even at that moment, as he walked briskly toward his new work at Miss Fuller's school, in a far corner of his mind other plans were beginning to take form. "Perhaps," he thought, "even though my days are filled with teaching, I will be able to go on with my experiments in vibrations. I could set up my tuning forks in my bedroom and work on them in the evening. There is so much about the vibrations of the air that is not known yet."

He paused to let a cart piled high with silver mackerel pass in front of him.

"Speech, after all, is nothing but a vibration, a movement of the air," he reflected. "If I experiment long enough, I ought to be able to make vowel sounds with my tuning forks, and consonant sounds too. And then I'd have words— maybe I could send them along an electric wire. I think the German, Helmholtz, did something like that. At least it seemed that way to me from the illustrations in the book I saw. I couldn't read the German. . . ."

The sea wind, blowing along the street, tugged at his muffler.

"Whether he did it or not, maybe I could do it. . . . It would be a wonderful thing to make words and send them along a wire."

So he walked on, and came at last to Pemberton Square, and paused before a rather stately front door over which "Eleven" was written in handsome gilt script. There he stopped long enough to take the letter from his pocket as if it were a calling card, then mounted the front steps and pulled the brass knob of the bell. After the doorbell had jingled, Miss Sarah Fuller herself opened the front door.

"Come in, Mr. Bell," she said. "I'm so glad you're here. It seems as if all Boston wants to know more about teaching by visible speech. . . . We expect great things of you, Mr. Bell."

And she led him up the wide red-carpeted stairs to his room.

"You'll have plenty of time to get unpacked and settled," she said. "Dinner is not till twelve, and your classes won't begin till Monday. Later we'll find you another place to board."

Aleck looked at the modest leather-covered bag that held his belongings.

"Thank you. I'll be ready at twelve," he said.

On Monday morning his work began. And after that, day after day, he stood before his class while the children watched or felt the movements of his lips and tried to imitate them. Sometimes he held up charts showing symbols of how their lips should be placed and watched each child making brave efforts to pronounce the words he or she could not hear. Aleck had some private pupils too and gave a good many lectures to teachers. The days went very fast for him.

But though he liked his teaching and grew fond of the pupils who were sent to him, the evenings were the time he looked forward to. Then, with his tuning forks set up in his bedroom, he experimented with vibrations of the air. After a while he had the idea of getting the tuning forks going with electromagnets—metal bars wrapped with wire and made magnetic by an electric current—and then of picking up the vibrations with other tuning forks set at the end of an electric wire.

"I believe I could send messages that way," he said to himself one night. "A kind of harmonic telegraph."

So it was that Alexander Graham Bell started his career as a teacher of the deaf, and all the while the thought of sending words along a wire was in his mind.

2
Mr. Bell
Meets Mr. Watson

"Lord!" said Thomas Watson, looking up from his workbench in Charles Williams' Electrical Shop. "Another of these inventors!" He did not say it aloud, for Alexander Graham Bell stood before him, but he said it to himself, quite heatedly. "Another of these inventors, always thinking they have new ideas that no one in the world has ever thought of before, always thinking that they will make great fortunes . . ."

To Bell he said, "Is there anything

wrong with the model I have made you?"

Charles Williams' Electrical Shop, to which Bell came that afternoon, was on Court Street in Boston. It was a place that many inventors visited in the 1870s to have working models of their inventions made. A big dusty room it was, with whitewashed walls, a confusion of lathes and whirring belts, a great heap of scrap iron, and a forge for annealing metal. About twenty-five men were working at their benches there, and one of the most skilled of them was Thomas Watson.

He was only about twenty that morning in 1874 when he first met Alexander Graham Bell, but he had already done many kinds of work, for he had had to leave school when he was only twelve. He had been an errand boy, a dishwasher, a waiter. But at last he had come to Williams' shop, drawn there perhaps because electricity had such a fascination for him. His fingers were uncommonly deft, his brain uncommonly quick, and he had soon built up a reputation among inventors because of the perfection of the models he made. Williams talked of someday making him a foreman.

Now Watson looked up from the work he was doing and saw Bell standing before him, a part of the model for a harmonic telegraph in his hand. Pale, slender, hazel-eyed, with a warm plaid muffler tied around his neck, Bell had come directly to Watson's bench, ignoring the usual practice of taking all complaints to the office of the shop.

"Is there something wrong?" Watson asked.

"Yes," Bell said. "It's not right. This part—I'm sure it won't work."

Watson took the model in question, noticing as he did so Bell's hazel eyes, the dark hair that lay on either cheek in the sideburns customary for gentlemen of the day, and the clothes, well cut and of good fabric, though they were a little worn. Watson was used to the society of laboring men, and he found Bell interesting.

Watson began, "I've made it this way, because from all my study of electricity it would seem—"

Bell flashed a quick look at him.

"You've studied electricity?" Bell said. "Then you'll know what I am trying to do. I'm going to make what I call a harmonic telegraph—one that will make it possible to send several messages over the same wire at the same time. It will be done, you see, by means of tuning forks, each one vibrating at a different pitch. It will be a great, important invention, I'm sure of that. But there are some points about it that I have not been able to work out." There was a shadow on his face. "Maybe you could help me, Mr. Watson."

Watson smiled. "Of course I'll help you in any way I can," he said. He forgot what he had been thinking about inventors, with their grand ideas of making fortunes. "I should think your idea was a very good one. If you could set the tuning forks vibrating, send the vibrations along a wire, and then have another set of tuning forks at the other end, and time them exactly . . ."

"That's it," Bell said.

Around them the machinery clattered

and clanked, chains rattled, hammers pounded. But Bell and Watson ignored all that. On a small stool, close to Watson's workbench, Bell sat down. Pulling out a notebook from his pocket, the inventor began to sketch.

"It would be like this," he said.

"No, Mr. Bell," Watson said. "This would be the way to do it, wouldn't it?"

They talked on and on, the excitement of the new invention stimulating them like wine.

At length they were conscious that the activity around them had died down. Workmen at the neighboring benches were putting their tools away.

"It must be six o'clock," Watson said. "It's closing time."

Bell stood up. He felt as if their talk had only just begun.

"Why don't you come over to my boardinghouse, Mr. Watson?" he said. "We could have supper there."

If there were others at the boardinghouse table, Bell and Watson were oblivious of them. Neither one remembered afterward what he had eaten. Only Watson wrote later in his autobiography that he noticed how deftly Bell ate with a fork. Watson had never before sat at a table where forks were used.

After supper was over, they sat down in the boardinghouse parlor where the beaded curtains and the dried straw flowers were. A piano stood in one corner, draped with a deep-fringed silken shawl.

"Do you play?" Bell asked, and Watson shook his head. He did not say that he could not play and also did not know a single person who could.

Bell sat down at the piano and let his fingers move across the keys. Once, when he was a little boy, he had thought that he would be a musician, and though he had given up that ambition long ago, he still loved music. Soon the rippling notes of a Chopin prelude filled the parlor, and Watson listened, marveling.

So it was that Mr. Bell and Mr. Watson found each other.

3
"I've Had
Another Idea"

After that, Aleck Bell and Tom Watson worked together on the harmonic telegraph. They usually made their experiments in the evening after the employees in the electrical shop had gone home. For Aleck was still trying to earn his living by teaching deaf pupils to speak, and Tom Watson was kept busy all day with his model making. But the evenings were their own.

Charles Williams had no objection to their using the attic of his electrical shop on Court Street for their laboratory, and they often worked there until after midnight. All through the spring of 1875 they worked together in the attic trying to make the harmonic telegraph.

One night it seemed hotter there than they had ever known it, but they paid little attention, so involved were they in what they had to do. They did not hear the carts of noisy party-goers clattering home over the cobblestones below them, nor the watchman with his rattle, nor even the mosquitoes that came singing at the windows. They worked in silence, barely speaking to each other.

At one end of the attic Watson stood, a row of tuning forks before him, and some batteries and some coiled electromagnets. Some distance away, at the other end of the attic, Aleck stood behind another assortment of tuning forks. A long wire stretched between the two men.

From time to time Aleck took up a tuning fork and held it close to his ear. Then he put it down, made a slight adjustment, and tried it again.

But nothing seemed to go right that night. They knew their theory was correct, but they could not make it work. The notes they sent along the wire, although carefully tuned, were continually jumbled together. They tried and tried again, and finally they grew tired from the heat and their long hours of work. For the first time since he had been working at the device, Bell felt discouraged. It grew later and later, and the sounds over their wires seemed more and more confused.

Aleck sat down on a rough bench near the window, trying to get a breath of fresher air. Watson stopped too and came over to join him. Out in the street the gas lamp sent a hot yellow glow into the dark.

"I don't know, Mr. Watson," Bell said. "There are others working on harmonic telegraphs. I don't know whether we will be able to perfect this one before they get their patents or not."

Watson smiled. "I never heard you talk like that before, Mr. Bell," he said. "How many times have you come into the shop saying, 'Mr. Watson, we're on the verge of a great discovery!' In all the weeks we've worked together, I've never heard you doubt it."

"I know," Bell said. The two men looked out into the darkness of Court Street.

Watson was first to break the silence. He rose and went back toward the tuning forks. "I'll just try them once more," he said.

Bell sat still for a few minutes, then he turned from the window. "Wait a minute, Mr. Watson," he said. "There's another thing. . . . I don't think I ever told you about it. I have another idea, and if it works . . ." Watson noticed an unusual quality in Bell's voice, as if he were talking in a dream.

"I think if we could get current that varied in intensity as air waves vary with sound—if we could get a current of that kind, I'm almost sure we could send sounds along a wire and receive them on a sort of eardrum, made of metal, maybe. Do you see what I mean? If we could do that, people in distant places could talk to each other. We could send *speech* along a wire, not just the dots and dashes of the Morse code."

Watson considered. It was an astounding thing that Mr. Bell had proposed. It all depended, of course, on whether they could create the kind of current they wanted.

"I should think it could be done," Watson said at last. "But I don't know enough about electricity to know how such a current could be made."

"Neither do I," Bell said. "But I'll show you how I thought we could make the sending and receiving instruments. The sending would not be so hard, but the thing that received the varying current would be harder. Come over here and let me show you."

They went to a table under a flickering gas jet. "Now suppose the transmitter was something like this," Bell said. He drew a sheet of paper toward him and began to draw.

"That wouldn't be so hard to make," Watson said, grasping the details of what

Bell drew. "That could be done. But the thing would have to be very big, so that you could make every sound of the human voice. I should think it would have to be about as big as a grand piano."

"Yes, I guess it would," Bell said. Mr. Watson was certainly quick to grasp details, once an idea was given him, Bell thought.

He said aloud, "Let's make it as big as a grand piano, then. Maybe some time in the future we could find a way to make it smaller."

"Probably we could," Watson agreed, taking up the sketch and examining it closely.

"Have you thought of the question of expense?" he went on. "I can't figure it out exactly, of course, until the model has been made, but offhand I should think it would cost a good many hundred dollars."

A good many hundred dollars! Mr. Bell, the elocution teacher in his well-cut threadbare coat, looked at Mr. Watson, the mechanic, earning his weekly wages at Williams' Electrical Shop.

"I suppose it would," Bell said. "Maybe we'd better just set it aside for the present. I only thought it might be an interesting idea. Let's see if we can't make this thing work."

The two young men turned back to their tuning forks.

But the idea of a current that might carry voices along a wire to people listening in distant places persisted. Try as he might, Bell could not rid himself of it. At last he thought, "Suppose it does cost a lot of money. There are people who have a lot of money. Perhaps they would be willing to back it."

A day or two later Bell mustered up his courage and called on Mr. Hubbard and Mr. Sanders, the two Boston financiers who were paying the expenses of his harmonic telegraph. Would they be interested in backing his work on the telephone, he asked them. Both men answered no. At that time they could see no future for the telephone instrument that Bell described.

The harmonic telegraph was another matter. Western Union was building telegraph lines right across the country. It was taking messages faster than it could possibly send them. If Bell continued work on the harmonic telegraph, Western Union would furnish some money for the materials he needed. He had better not waste any time on other experiments, though. Other men were said to be working on harmonic telegraphs. Mr. Bell had better take his specifications to Washington at once and have them registered at the United States Patent Office.

Bell thanked the Western Union men and prepared to go to Washington with the patent specifications for the harmonic telegraph in his pocket.

4

A Young Inventor
Calls On
an Older One

When he had finished his work at the Patent Office in Washington, Bell made his way to the Smithsonian Institution. It was a raw, blustery day in March, and he pulled his plaid wool muffler close around his neck and plunged his hands down into his pockets. "Washington is a good many miles south of Boston, but that doesn't mean it's any warmer," he thought.

Joseph Henry was the director of the

Smithsonian Institution then. He was eighty years old and a great physicist— one of the greatest physicists in the world. There were a number of questions Bell wanted to ask him about the harmonic telegraph.

Fortunately there was no difficulty about seeing him. Bell did not even have to wait.

"Come in," Joseph Henry said after his secretary had brought Bell to the door. "Won't you sit down? I want very much to hear about your invention."

Bell took the chair that Joseph Henry motioned toward, set his hat down on a nearby table, began to untie his muffler, and looked across the wide desk at the slender old gentleman with the narrow, stooping shoulders and the keen eyes.

"I'm always so glad to have young inventors come here," Dr. Henry said. "It's a good many years since I have done any scientific experimenting myself, but I remember when I was working at my electric motor what a help it was to talk it over." He paused and took a large silk handkerchief from his pocket. "I have a very bad cold," he said.

Then Bell began to explain to him about the harmonic telegraph, and the vibrations of his tuning forks, and his idea that various vibrations could be sent over a wire at the same time. Joseph Henry followed what he said without interruption.

"I'd like to see your harmonic telegraph," he said at last.

"I have a small model of it in my hotel bedroom," Bell said, pleased that Joseph Henry should be so interested.

The scientist rose and walked toward the coatrack, where his coat and hat were hanging.

"I'd like very much to see it," he said. "I could go right over. Where are you staying?"

"Oh, but I could bring it here tomorrow," the younger man answered. "It's so blustery outside. And you have such a cold."

So it was arranged that Bell would come again the next morning and bring his model with him. And Joseph Henry went home to a large hot toddy and mustard footbath. But his cold did not prevent him from keeping his appointment the next day.

The harmonic telegraph operated better than it had ever done in Williams' shop. As they worked together—the great physicist with his record of achievement known to scientists throughout the world, and the young man whose achievements still lay before him—a strong bond of sympathy was established between the two.

Bell lingered on after his demonstration was over and his model was packed in his bag. At last, just as he was beginning to reach for his muffler, he paused.

"There is another thing," he said. "Another idea I've had. You may not think it is worth anything."

"What is it?" Henry asked, smiling because the young man seemed so shy.

Then, in a voice that was low but intense, Bell briefly explained his idea of sending a human voice along a wire.

"If I could do it, people would be able to converse together across miles of space. . . ."

He looked at Dr. Henry, wondering whether the idea would seem absurd to him, as it had to Mr. Hubbard and Mr. Sanders.

But the older man had risen from his chair and was walking toward Bell with his hand out.

"I think you have the germ of a great invention," he said. "An idea that would change the world, as only a few inventions have ever done."

Bell drew a deep breath. "There's only one difficulty," he said. "I am not really a scientist. I am a teacher of elocution. I do not know much about electricity. The person who works out that idea ought to know electrical theory. . . . Would it be better, do you think, to publish the idea and let some scientist develop it?"

An expression of indignation crossed Joseph Henry's kindly face.

"What nonsense!" he said. "Did I broadcast my idea about the electric motor and let some other man develop it because I did not know how it could be done? What man wants to miss the satisfaction of making a great invention, simply because he will not study the theory by which it can be accomplished? If you don't have sufficient knowledge of electricity to make the thing, *then get it.*"

He pulled his great silk handkerchief from his pocket and applied it to his nose.

5
Within Reach
of a Discovery

One evening every week Aleck would take the horsecar and go to Brattle Street to call on Mabel Hubbard. Her father, who had liked the young man ever since Bell had consulted him about the telegraph, had decided to bring his daughter to Aleck for help in diction. She had lost her hearing when at age four she had scarlet fever. Her parents had hired someone to teach her lip reading, a new thing in America then, and had taken her to Germany for further instruction. Still, at the age of sixteen, though she could form words and read lips perfectly, she had some difficulty controlling her voice.

"Her mother and I would be most grateful if you could give her some help," Mr. Hubbard had said to Aleck. Aleck had promised to do everything he could.

After a few weeks there was no longer much need of Aleck's teaching, for Mabel spoke very well. Still, he continued to go to the Hubbard house every week. He felt somehow at home there.

Gradually, although he was twenty-six and Mabel Hubbard only sixteen, an understanding grew between them. They knew that someday they would marry.

"As soon as I can earn enough," he would say to her. "As soon as we have enough to live on . . ."

"It wouldn't take much, would it?" she would say.

And he would answer, "No, not much. But more than we have now."

On the evening after his return from Washington, he took the horsecar to Brattle Street as usual, but that night his heart was very heavy. He wanted so much to marry—and he had scarcely any money at all. There was only one way of making it, he knew. His elocution lessons would never earn enough. But if he could perfect the harmonic telegraph, surely then he would have enough. Both Mr. Hubbard and Mr. Sanders believed there was a great future for it. So, he said to himself, he would work on the harmonic telegraph. It needed a great deal more experimenting before it was perfected.

But if he did this, what would happen to his idea of the telephone? It was the telephone that he was really interested in. And Joseph Henry had thought so much of it! Well, he might as well give up thinking about the telephone now and go to work on the harmonic telegraph. There wasn't any other way.

He talked very little about his trip to Washington that night and scarcely mentioned Joseph Henry. There wasn't any use in letting Mabel know that the director of the Smithsonian was interested in his telephone. He wasn't going to make a telephone after all. He was going to perfect the harmonic telegraph.

Mabel thought he looked very tired when he said good night to her that night.

"Try not to work so hard, Aleck," she said. "Can't you manage to get a little more sleep?"

The next day Aleck set to work with Watson in the attic of Williams' shop. He gave up his teaching temporarily to have more time for his experiments on the harmonic telegraph. The wire was strung from one attic room to another, a distance of about sixty feet.

Sometime before this they had found the tuning forks unsatisfactory, and Aleck had decided to try steel organ reeds in place of them. Each organ reed vibrated over an electromagnet.

"This is much better," he had said to Watson. "The vibrations are longer, and we can tune them more accurately."

So they began using organ reeds, not tuning forks, and they soon discovered they could set them vibrating with only one electromagnet.

Their harmonic telegraph looked like this:

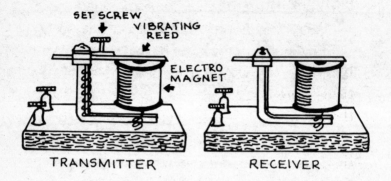

Watson, at one end of the long wire, started the reed vibrating and tuned it with a setscrew. Bell, at the other end, tuned the receiver and held his ear close to it to catch the sound of the vibrations. His musical ear was quick to catch variations in pitch. Day after day they worked that way, all through the spring.

Then, one day, on June 2, 1875, after they had been experimenting a long time, there was a pause in the vibrations over the wire. Bell listened, but no sound came. One of the organ reeds on Watson's transmitting instrument had stuck.

It was then that Watson gave the stuck

reed a tweak with his finger. And Bell heard a sound coming over the wire that he had never heard before.

He ran to the place where Watson stood.

"What did you do?" he asked, his eyes burning with excitement. "Leave everything exactly as it is. Don't change anything. That's the current we want!"

Afterward they understood clearly what had happened. The timing screw had been too closely adjusted, and it had prevented the usual strong current from going through the wire. Then the faint current, passing between the vibrating steel organ reed and the electromagnet, could be heard. In that moment Bell's delicate ear had caught the sound of an undulating current—a current that varied in intensity, like the sound waves of a human voice.

"It's right!" Bell said, triumph in his voice. "It's exactly what we want. If that sound can travel along the wire, so can a voice. We have only to perfect it. The thing we're looking for is here!"

Suddenly the heat of the attic room was forgotten. Their tiredness, the difficulty with the harmonic telegraph—what did they matter? Now they knew that the great discovery was within their reach.

Again and again they tried to repeat the accident. Again and again Bell could hear the faint undulating current when the transmitter spring was plucked.

"Let's design a transmitter and a receiver especially for the undulating current," Bell said at last. "We'll make them simple at first, then perfect them later. Can you work on the models tomorrow? Can you rush them through?"

"How will we make them?" Watson asked.

And Bell drew a paper across the table and began to sketch. "Like this," he said. "We can mount a small drumhead of gold leaf over one of the receivers, like this. And we can join the center of the drumhead to the free end of the receiving spring and make a mouthpiece over the drumhead to talk into."

"That shouldn't be hard to do," Watson replied. "I think I could have it ready by tomorrow night."

"We'll leave it at that then," Bell said. "We can't do any more tonight."

So they turned out the gas and went down the stairs and out past the deserted workbenches of Williams' shop. At the door they paused. Watson took a key from his pocket and carefully locked the door.

"Good night then, Mr. Watson. Until tomorrow night," Aleck said.

"Good night, Mr. Bell," Watson answered. And they parted, going in different ways.

But Aleck could not go straight to bed. He walked quickly along the darkened streets, farther and farther, until at last he had gone all the way to Brattle Street. In the Hubbard house there were no lights. Every window was darkened.

At last he turned, walked slowly back to the room where he lived, and got into bed. But when morning came he had not slept.

6

"I Could Almost Understand the Words!"

The model that Watson made was ready the next day. Excited, they carried it to the attic and attached it to the wire they had been using for the harmonic telegraph. Then, Watson at one end of the wire and Bell at the other, they prepared to try it. But the rooms were so small that they heard each other's voices anyway: they could not tell whether their words were passing along the wire or not.

"I could carry the wire down the stairs and attach it to my workbench," Watson said. "Then we couldn't hear each other's voices through the air."

So he got a long coil of wire and extended it down two flights of stairs, and soon they were ready to try again.

Now from his post in the attic Bell shouted into the receiver, directing his voice toward the center of the diaphragm (a thin membrane). Then he stopped and held the instrument to his ear, listening for Watson's answering voice. But he heard no sound along the wire. There was only silence.

He tried again. "What is wrong?" he wondered. He sang and whistled and then held the instrument up to his ear once more. Again there was silence. The walls of the attic seemed to press in around him. The heat was intense. A trickle of sweat ran down his forehead. What could be wrong? He was almost sure that the instrument had been correctly made.

Then as he stood there, looking at the silent instrument, he heard a clatter on the stairs, and Watson came rushing into the room.

"I heard you!" Watson was crying. "I heard you plainly. I could almost understand the words!"

So their theory had been right. It would be possible to send speech along a wire. But no one could have known better than they that long days of experimenting lay ahead of them. They were prepared for that.

They didn't want to go on with their experiments that afternoon where anyone might see them. It was about suppertime anyway. So they hid their instrument in Watson's clothes locker and went out to have a meal together. In the evening, after all the men had left, they returned to Williams' empty shop, took their telephone from Watson's locker, and began to work in earnest.

7
Overwork

"I saw your father last night and told him about the telephone, but he would hardly listen to me," Aleck said to Mabel a few days later. "I told him that it meant twenty times as much to the world as the harmonic telegraph, and that I wanted to spend all my time perfecting it—but he wouldn't listen. He said he had invested his money in developing the harmonic telegraph, and that was what must be completed."

Mabel Hubbard did not answer. She knew her father's stubbornness, but she

thought she knew that there was stubbornness in Aleck too. Sitting in a corner
of the horsehair sofa, she worked carefully
at a piece of multicolored embroidery. Bell
sat opposite her on a straight-backed wal-
nut chair. The afternoon sun came in
through the long lace curtains at the window, lighting her brown curls and Bell's
pale earnest face.

"There was another thing," he said at
last. "You may as well know it now as
later." Mabel's eyes intently watched his
lips. "Your father said that if I persisted in
attempting such a crazy scheme, he would
forbid our marriage."

Mabel put down her embroidery. "He
couldn't do that," she said. "When two
grown people want to marry, there is no
way of stopping them." She smiled. "I
think my mother will help us."

"Then I think I'll give it a try," Aleck
said. And that in fact was what he did.

Work on the harmonic telegraph was set
aside now. His elocution classes had already been given up. He was not sure exactly how he would manage to live, but it

did not matter. He was committed to the telephone now.

Since it seemed necessary that the work should be kept secret, at least for the present, two rooms in a boardinghouse at Exeter Place were rented. Aleck used one of them for his bedroom, the other for his laboratory.

Watson too was fired with enthusiasm for the new invention. He set aside his work at Williams' shop and gave all his time to the telephone. They worked all day and late into the night.

The rooms in the boardinghouse cost only three dollars a week, and that was fortunate. There was little money for food and scarcely any time to eat. But these things did not matter. Hour after hour, day and night, Bell and Watson worked at testing and experimenting.

"You must get some sleep," Mabel told him, coming up the stairs to see him one day. But Aleck said he had no time for sleep, kissed her lightly, and turned back to his work.

After that she did not come to his workroom for three days. Then he heard her footsteps on the stairs, and when he opened the door he saw that she was standing on the landing with a package under her arm.

"It's your portrait," she said, holding it out to him. "See if you like it."

Bell's fingers fumbled with the string a little, but soon the wrappings were torn off, and he held it out at arm's length.

"My portrait?" he said, and a broad smile broke across his serious face. For there he saw a night owl with soft barred feathers and bright eyes. He set it on the mantelpiece and looked at it and laughed.

"I have to work that way now," he said. "I have to be a night owl. Later, you know, there will be more time."

Mabel lingered on a little and then left him. For she knew as well as he did that their future together depended on the work Bell did in his laboratory that summer.

Through July the days and nights grew hotter and hotter. And then in August it began to rain. Day after day and night after night it rained. The hot, dreary rain fell on the Boston streets and drenched the houses, but it brought no relief from the stifling heat. Yet Bell and Watson worked on in their hot room.

It was in September that Bell fell sick. He was standing near the window, testing a receiver drum, when suddenly it seemed to him that the room was swinging around him, and a roaring that had nothing to do with the telephone filled his ears. He felt himself fall to the floor, and a blackness seemed to swallow him. And the next thing he knew, Watson was bending over him.

"I'll get you into bed," Watson was saying. "The heat has been too much." Bell, feeling limp as a child, managed to get to bed with Watson's help before the blackness came down around him again.

"He must have a long rest," the doctor said next morning. "Is there anyone who can take care of him?"

"I'll look after him," Watson said, looking down at his friend, who lay limp and helpless in his bed. "Tell me just what to do, and I'll see that it's done."

"For a few days he ought to stay perfectly quiet here," the doctor said. "Then
if he could have some country air, and
plenty of sleep and good food . . ."

No one could have been gentler than
Watson in those next few days. Tirelessly
he bathed Bell's aching forehead with cool
water and drew the blinds to keep the sun
away from his patient's eyes. He made
charts with scientific accuracy so that the
doctor would know exactly what food had
been given, and he recorded temperatures
to the fraction of a degree.

And every day Mabel Hubbard
mounted the stairs, remaining only long
enough to assure herself that the patient
had progressed a little since the day before.

Gradually Bell grew stronger. Before very
long he was able to sit propped up in bed,
and then with Watson's help he could
walk into the workroom, where the aban-
doned wires of the telephone were
stretched.

"You mustn't work on it yet," Watson

said. "The doctor says you must have a long rest before you go back to work."

Bell agreed to wait, feeling indeed very little desire to take up the work that had absorbed him so before his illness.

It was arranged that he should go to his parents' home in Canada to get well again. He drove in a horse-drawn cab to the station, a few shirts and socks in his bag, together with a collection of notebooks with sketches for his telephone. Although he was to spend several months resting, still there were things he could do with the telephone. He wanted to try stringing wires from fence posts so that he could make further experiments with his instrument. He would also be able to work on the description of his invention so that it could be sent to the patent attorneys in Washington.

By March 7, 1876, the patent for the first telephone was granted to Bell, and he was back at work in his rooms at 5 Exeter Place that same month. That year he was twenty-nine years old.

8

"Mr. Watson, Come Here"

Sometimes the telephone worked pretty well; sometimes it didn't. Watson could usually hear Bell's voice on it, although he could not make out the words. Bell could hardly ever hear Watson at all.

"We've got to perfect it, Mr. Watson," Bell kept saying. "It's got to work better than this if it is to be any good at all."

Over and over they tried it. Sometimes the sounds came along the wires, sometimes not. They decided to try a new kind of transmitter. But how could they make it, they wondered. What kind of instrument would send the undulating current that they wanted along the wire?

Bell invented one at last. He attached the wire to a diaphragm, and let the wire touch diluted acid in a metal cup. When the sound of a voice made the diaphragm vibrate, the depth of the wire in the acid varied, and so the resistance of the circuit varied. Then the current that ran along the wire vibrated like the undulating sound of the human voice. Bell knew when he made it that it was an improvement on the instrument he had made before. But there were so many chances for error. He waited nervously while Watson worked on the model from his drawings.

Watson brought the new transmitter to the laboratory in Exeter Place early in the evening. "Maybe it will work better," he said cheerfully. "At any rate, we have all night to experiment with it."

He attached the transmitter to the wires. Bell went into his bedroom and took his place beside the bureau where the transmitter was set. Watson put his ear to the receiver. There was a long pause.

Then suddenly, as clearly as if he were standing beside him, he heard Bell's voice. And not only the voice, but also Bell's words could be understood. Every syllable was as clear and distinct as if he were in the small room.

"Mr. Watson," the voice was saying, "come here. I want you." Amazed, Watson held the instrument for a moment. He had never heard Bell's voice so clearly over that wire before. He put the telephone down and ran into the other room. A bowl of sulfuric acid had been overturned, and the burning liquid was running down Bell's clothes.

But Watson paid no attention to the spreading acid. "It was clear," he said. "I have never heard it so clear before. Every syllable, every tone. This is the way we must make it. This is the telephone. Try it again."

Whether Bell took off his acid-stained

clothes, whether or not he was burned, neither of them ever told. That did not seem to make any difference. What they remembered for years afterward was that statement, that call for help—"Mr. Watson, come here. I want you"—so clear, distinct, unmistakable.

"Let's try it again," Bell said. "You go back to the laboratory; I'll stand here." And in a moment he was holding the instrument to his lips again. "Can you hear me plainly?"

"Yes," came the answer. "I can hear you perfectly."

What can two young men say to each other over a telephone, over the first telephone in the world? Surely there ought to be some great sentences, some profound utterances. But they had thought of none. It did not matter what they said.

"One, two, three," Bell announced solemnly.

"Four, five, six," Watson answered clearly.

"God save the Queen," Bell continued.

So the night wore on. By morning they knew that they had made, much sooner than they had dared to hope, the instrument that would make it possible for people to carry on a conversation across miles of space.

9

The Emperor Dom Pedro Recognizes Mr. Bell

On the afternoon of June 24, 1876, Alexander Graham Bell walked through the Centennial Fair Grounds at Fairmount Park in Philadelphia. The model of the telephone had been sent on ahead. It was extremely hot, as Philadelphia often is at the end of June, and the bag that he carried seemed heavier than when he left Boston. He had had a long, uncomfortable journey and had taken time for only a cup of tea and a bun in the station so he might get to the Centennial Exposition before it closed for the day. He had been informed that the judges would inspect his telephone on Sunday morning, which was the next day.

At another time he might have lingered to look at the array of strange buildings past which he walked—the great Horticultural Hall built in the Moorish style of iron and glass, the Spanish and German and Portuguese pavilions, the Turkish café, and the Japanese gardens. But he was too tired to be interested in them; he had not wanted to come to the Centennial in the first place.

"Of course you ought to go," Mabel had told him. "You *must* exhibit the telephone there. All the great inventions of the century will be on exhibition—yours ought to be there too."

Just at that moment Mrs. Hubbard had joined in the conversation. "You'll have barely time to get a space in the exhibition at all," she said. "Mr. Hubbard says that the official entries are closed already. But I think he'll be able to get you in. Why don't you take Mabel's cousin Willie down to help you? Then Mr. Watson won't have to leave his work."

What chance had Aleck to stay home with two competent women persuading him to leave? He agreed to go. But he said he could not stay more than a few days.

Now he stood at the door of the great exhibition hall, a structure that covered twenty acres. He paused and drew his pass from his pocket. It was engraved like a bank note and bore his photograph, with the severe warning that it would be taken away if it was presented by any but the proper person. The guard at the door read it carefully. "A. G. Bell, Exhibitor; Country, U.S.; Class 8727; Signed: David G. Yates, General Manager of Admissions." Then he looked at the photograph, and he looked at Bell. "All right," he said and opened the admission gate.

Inside the hall Bell found himself a part of the stream of visitors. There were finely dressed ladies with narrow waists who wore bustled skirts, gay little hats, and parasols. And there were gentlemen with sideburns, swinging canes. They moved slowly down the aisles of the great hall, stopping to peer at printing presses, at exhibitions of pottery and glass, furs and furniture, looms and railroad locomotives. But Bell did not pause to look at any of these things. He made his way to the corner of the East Gallery where his exhibits would be set up.

Arranging the instruments did not take him long. The models that Mr. Watson had made specially for the exhibition were soon in order.

By the time the closing gong rang and the people had begun to leave the hall, everything was all ready—the wires, the metal cup filled with acid and water, the diaphragm. He had rigged the wire so that it stretched all the way across the exhibition hall. When all this was done, he set up a little sign, neatly lettered:

THE TELEPHONE

A. Graham Bell

Then he went to his hotel room for the night.

Next morning Willie Hubbard arrived, and together they went back to the East Gallery. Only exhibitors were allowed on Sunday morning. The great hall was very quiet when they entered. Here and there an exhibitor was making some last-minute adjustment to the things he had to show, but most of them sat idly waiting or chatting together.

Bell could think of nothing more that he could do with his instrument, so he and Willie Hubbard sat down in chairs beside it and waited. After a long time a bell sounded in the distance. At the far end of the hall a door was thrown open, and the judges entered in their stovepipe hats and long frock coats.

Bell and Willie Hubbard watched them across the length of the hall. Slowly, with long pauses before each exhibit, they came nearer. "That must be Lord Kelvin," Willie said excitedly. "The greatest scientist in the world today, they say he is. What a man for a judge!" Willie had been well informed about all the notables.

"There's Joseph Henry, that tall thin man. I saw him at the Smithsonian," Bell said.

"And who do you suppose that can be with him?" Willie asked. "That heavy man with the reddish hair and the square-cut beard?"

Bell peered across the hall. "Why, I know him," he said. "I've talked to him. He came up to the Boston School for the Deaf when I was teaching there. Wanted to know what methods we used. Talked a long time—or I did, rather." Bell smiled.

"But who is he?" Willie Hubbard asked, exasperated at all this talk when all he wanted was to be told a name.

"He comes from Brazil," Bell continued. "His name is Dom Pedro. He's the emperor."

"Dom Pedro!" Willie said. "Why didn't you say so? He's the guest of honor of the whole fair. His picture is hanging in all the streets of Philadelphia. They say there was a great picture of the emperor and the empress all lighted up with gaslights last night. . . . Did you say you'd talked to him?"

"Yes," Alexander said. "In Boston."

The judges were slowly coming toward them. They were near enough now to be plainly seen.

"They look awfully hot, don't they?" Willie said. "Hot and tired."

"It seems as if they are losing interest in the exhibits," Aleck answered. "I don't believe ours will look like much."

Now the judges had come to the exhibition of Swedish glass just beside the place where Bell and Willie Hubbard sat. They were so near that it was easy to hear what they were saying.

"Gentlemen," they heard Lord Kelvin saying in his clear-cut, aristocratic English voice, "if you will inspect this collection of glass from Sweden, we will pause in our considerations and continue with our judging tomorrow. This American heat makes it impossible . . ."

Bell looked at Willie Hubbard. "That's the end of that," he said. "Tomorrow I will be on the train to Boston. I've got to get back and start teaching again. Maybe it's just as well."

The judges had inspected the Swedish glass—not too carefully perhaps. Lord Kelvin turned to leave the hall. He paused and with customary ceremony waited for the emperor to precede him. But Dom Pedro, a man of curiosity and independence, did not turn immediately. He wanted to see what the small exhibit on the next table might be. He stopped for a moment and recognized Alexander Graham Bell, the pale face, the dark ruffled hair, the burning eyes.

"Why, Mr. Bell," he said. And in a moment he was striding toward him with outstretched hand. "How are things going in Boston?" he asked. "What is this you are showing here?"

Bell told him that he had brought a model of the telephone, and that he was sorry that it would not be judged, for it would be necessary for him to leave the next day. "I am sorry that the judges will not have an opportunity to see it," he said politely.

"But that's impossible," Dom Pedro said. "Of course they'll have to see it now. Lord Kelvin," he called, turning back to the impatient group of judges. "I must ask you to wait, gentlemen. This is Mr. Bell of Boston. He has made what he calls a telephone. He cannot wait until tomorrow to show it to us. We must see it now."

Wearily the judges turned. Even great scientists could not refuse the request of the emperor, who was also the guest of honor of the Centennial.

10
"Remarkable! Extraordinary!"

"Mr. Bell has an invention here which he calls the telephone." The voice of Dom Pedro held the judges as if against their will. There was nothing to prevent their leaving, but not one of them turned away.

"His telephone is a device by which a human voice may be carried along an electric wire, so that a person standing at the other end of the wire may hear the speaker as if he stood beside him."

The judges made no comment. Some of

them looked bored, and some unbelieving. Some of them looked merely hot.

"Will Mr. Bell demonstrate his telephone?" Lord Kelvin asked.

Aleck rose and, having nothing that seemed suitable to say, bowed. Willie Hubbard rose too and turned to the instrument on the table.

Then Aleck walked to the transmitter, which he had rigged at the far end of the exhibition hall, took up the instrument, and waited for the familiar hum and click that meant that Willie Hubbard had turned on the current. "All right, Willie," he called into the transmitter.

"It's ready," Willie said to the assembled gentlemen. "Your Majesty, will you begin?"

Dom Pedro stepped forward and took up the little metal box that Willie held out to him. "Hold it close to your ear," Willie said.

There was a moment's pause. Dom Pedro stood in rapt attention; the judges watched. Then suddenly a smile broke across his face, an expression of great surprise. "My God, it talks!" he said.

Then Lord Kelvin took the instrument.

" 'To be, or not to be,' " he murmured, as if he were repeating the words of some priest in a great cathedral. " 'That is the question.' " He took the small black box down from his ear and looked at it, then raised it to his other ear, and listened. " 'The slings and arrows of outrageous fortune,' " he murmured. "Extraordinary! Will you try it, sir?"

A third judge stepped forward and took the small box attached to its wire and placed it to his ear. " 'By opposing end them'—I can hear it quite plainly. There is no doubt about it."

One after another the judges forgot the heat, forgot that they wanted to go home. They passed the receiver from one to another, taking turns. It was a thing they had never dreamed would be possible—to hear a voice that came clearly from the far end of the exhibition hall; to hear every word, every syllable. "Remarkable," they kept saying. "Extraordinary."

"Let Lord Kelvin try talking," one of

them said at last. "Let him see if he can make his voice come over the wire like that."

Lord Kelvin turned and walked away across the hall. After about five minutes Professor Barker of the University of Pennsylvania took up the receiver. "Sir William is speaking," he said. "Listen, Your Majesty." And he passed the instrument to the red-haired emperor.

Slowly, solemnly, in a low voice Dom Pedro repeated, " 'To be, or not to be'— it's Lord Kelvin's voice."

The demonstration was soon over. Bell, with Lord Kelvin, came walking back to the little group of waiting judges. They clapped as they saw him approaching, then one after another they shook his hand.

"Remarkable! Extraordinary!" they kept saying to one another as they made their way at last through the doors of the exhibition hall. Dom Pedro lingered a little after the others had gone.

"It's the most remarkable thing in America," he said. "You have made an invention that will change the way people live all over the world. There isn't any doubt about your getting the award, of course." He smiled at the confused young man. "Better get back to Boston," he said kindly. "You'll hear from us again."

Several days later the announcement of the award arrived. With it came a letter from Lord Kelvin, and Bell read the words of the great scientist with what seemed like a quiver of electricity:

I need scarcely say I was astonished and delighted, as were others, including some other judges of our group, who witnessed the experiments and verified with their own ears the electric transmission of speech. This, perhaps the greatest marvel hitherto achieved by the electric telegraph, has been obtained by appliances of quite a homespun and rudimentary character. With somewhat more advanced plans and more powerful apparatus, we may confidently expect that Mr. Bell will give us the means of making voice and spoken words audible through the electric wire to an ear hundreds of miles distant.

"Rudimentary? Homespun?" said Mr.

Watson later when Bell showed him the letter. His workmanship had been as good as any man could accomplish. "There wasn't anything homespun about it."

11

"Of What Use Is Such an Invention?"

One afternoon in October 1876, Aleck bought a copy of the New York *Tribune* from an old woman who had a newsstand at the corner of Exeter Place. The paper still carried accounts of various exhibits at the Centennial although the exposition had been going all summer. He glanced through the paper as he walked along the street, and turned to the editorial page. There his eye was caught by an article on the telephone. He paused before the door of number 5 to read it:

Of what use is such an invention? Well, there may be occasions of state when it is necessary for officials who are far apart to talk with each other, without the interferences of an operator. Or some lover may wish to pop the question directly into the ear of a lady and hear for himself her reply, though miles away; it is not for us to guess how courtships will be conducted in the twentieth century. It is said that the human voice has been conveyed by this contrivance over a circuit of sixty miles. Music can be readily transmitted. Think of serenading by telegraph!

Aleck gave the paper an angry shake and started running up the stairs three steps at a time.

"Read this, Mr. Watson," he cried, bursting into the room where Watson was experimenting with electromagnets. "Just read this. They want to know what use a telephone is!"

Watson took the paper and read. "I know," he said soberly. "I have heard people talk. They say that the telephone is an ingenious toy. Oh, they acknowledge that it can be used in a laboratory. And they have heard how you talked over the wires you strung along the fence posts in Canada last summer. But they don't see how it could be used commercially. Maybe the telegraph people don't want them to see."

"Then we'll have to make them see," Bell said.

᭏᭄ᭅ᭄᭏

The Walworth Manufacturing Company had an office on Kilby Street in Boston and a factory in Cambridgeport about two miles away. A private telegraph line connected the two. On October 9 Bell got permission to use this private line late in the afternoon after the office and factory were closed for the day.

"You take the apparatus out to Cambridgeport on the horsecar," he said to Watson. "I'll stay in the Boston office. We'll see if we can have a two-way conversation. Take a notebook and write down what you say and what you hear me answer. I'll do the same thing. That ought to convince people that our telephone might be some use in business."

It was beginning to grow dark when Watson reached the factory. He found the handle of a bell and pulled it. The sound of the jangling reached him.

He waited. After a while he heard footsteps. A watchman with a lantern opened the door. "What is it?" he said.

Watson explained that he had permission from the manager of the factory to try an experiment with the telephone on the company's telegraph line. "Can you tell me where the telegraph instrument is?" he asked.

The watchman grunted and motioned to Watson to come inside. He locked the door, and Watson followed him along the hall in the light of the lantern. At length they came to the great factory workroom, and the watchman put down his lantern, pulled matches from his pocket, and lighted the gas in several fixtures. The gas jets made a whistling sound before they burst into fan-shaped yellow flames.

"Can you show me where the telegraph outlet is?" Watson said again, observing to himself that the watchman had not said a single word since he had entered the building.

"It's over there," the watchman said, breaking the silence. "Have a care that you don't hurt it in any way."

Watson walked to the place the watchman indicated, opened his case, removed his tools, and lifted out the telephone instrument. It was the work of only a few minutes to disconnect the telegraph and connect the telephone. The watchman stood, his lantern still in his hand, an expression of distrust on his face.

"Now it ought to be all right," Watson said, as much to himself as to his close-mouthed guide. He pulled a large gold watch from his pocket to check the time. "Mr. Bell promised to be ready at eight o'clock."

Then he lifted the transmitter to his lips and called into it, "Ahoy! Ahoy there, Mr. Bell!" But when he held the receiver to his ear and listened, not the faintest sound came to him.

"That's strange," he murmured. And then he shouted, louder than before,

"Ahoy! Ahoy! Ahoy there, Mr. Bell! Are you there, Mr. Bell?"

Again he listened, and again there was silence.

The watchman, who was leaning against a post, pulled his pipe from his pocket and lighted it.

"Is that what you call a telephone?" he asked. "Think it's a useful contraption, do ye?"

Watson resisted a strong impulse to throw the instrument at the watchman's head. He leaned down, examined the electromagnets carefully, and pulled gingerly at the connecting wires. Everything seemed to be all right. He looked at his watch again—ten minutes after eight. He knew that Bell must be shouting into the telephone by this time. He shouted himself, and the sound echoed around the shadowy factory. Nothing. There was no response: nothing but dismal silence. He saw the watchman smiling scornfully.

What could the matter be, he wondered. Was it possible that a telephone that would work perfectly between two rooms could not be made to operate over wires that reached two miles? And why? Was it possible that the glass insulators that were satisfactory for the telegraph current were not right for the telephone? Did a little of the current he used leak to the ground at every support so that none of the electric undulations of Bell's voice got across the Charles River?

Watson's fingers worked deftly at the connections, and in his mind a dozen possible explanations for the failure presented themselves and were rejected. Then suddenly a thought occurred to him.

"Are there any other telegraph instruments in the building?" he asked the watchman sharply. "Another telegraph instrument would interfere with the current enough to make it impossible to use the telephone."

The watchman said he really did not know whether or not there were any others.

"Then we'll have to find out," Watson said. "Show me where the wire enters the building, and I'll trace along it and see."

Sulkily the watchman led the way with his lantern. It was plain enough to him that the whole telephone affair was some sort of humbug. Watson traced the wire along the factory wall and up some stairs. At last they came to a closed door.

"What's in there?" Watson asked.

The watchman drew a bunch of keys from his pocket, selected one of them, and fitted it into the lock. The door opened, and he lighted an ornate brass chandelier. "Office of the plant manager," he said.

Watson looked around. There it was. Over in the corner on a table, a telegraph instrument.

It was the work of only a moment to disconnect it. Then he turned and ran down the dark stairs, the watchman panting after him.

"Ahoy! Ahoy! Mr. Bell, are you there?" Watson called into the telephone.

He heard Bell's answer, clear, crisp, and sharp. "Where have you been?" Bell was shouting. "What have you been doing?" Never in all their experiments had Watson heard a voice so clearly. Every word, every syllable, every tone, precise and definite as if Bell were standing beside him. He had never heard Bell's voice so clearly when the telephone was connected from one room to another, and here it was stretching for two miles, and across a river. He could even tell that Mr. Bell was hoarse; he must have been shouting for a long time.

Then they began a conversation: the first long-distance telephone conversation that had ever been held. From time to time they paused, and each wrote down in his notebook what he had heard so that the notebooks could be compared later, and the record could be sent to the newspapers as proof that the telephone could work over two miles of space.

Watson asked Bell what time it was by his watch, and Bell told him. Then Bell asked Watson to try whispering, and Bell found that he could hear the whispering, though he could not understand the words. After a while Watson invited the watchman to listen, and the watchman did listen, rather grumpily.

Then finally they decided that they had

talked enough, and they put their precious notebooks into their pockets. Watson disconnected the telephone and connected the two telegraph instruments again. He packed up his tools and his telephone and followed the gloomy watchman to the door.

He walked back to Boston, striding down the deserted streets and over the bridge that spanned the Charles, and fairly ran up the stairs at 5 Exeter Place.

"Now they'll believe it! Now they'll have to believe it!" Bell called as Watson rushed into the room.

Watson said, "I heard you plainly. I heard every single word, over two miles, across the river! When the newspapers come out tomorrow, people will stop saying that the telephone is no use!"

"Come on, Mr. Watson," Bell said then. "A war dance is in order." And grasping the breathless Watson by both hands, he began to whirl him around the attic, knocking over tables and chairs, stamping and shouting as he went, unmindful of the sleeping lodgers on the floors below.

Next morning the landlady encountered Mr. Watson on the stairs. "I don't know what you are doing up there in the attic," she said, scowling. "But I cannot have my other roomers disturbed by your noisy goings-on in the middle of the night. I'll have to ask you and Mr. Bell to give up your rooms."

"I am so sorry," Mr. Watson answered. "Mr. Bell and I did not intend to disturb anyone. We were celebrating, but I am sure that we shall not do it again." He bowed politely, and the landlady swept angrily past him.

"I am perfectly sure we shall never celebrate just that again," he thought to himself. "No one will ever again have occasion to celebrate the first long-distance telephone conversation—of course, there may be other celebrations."

12

"We Cannot Use an Electrical Toy"

Sunday dinner at the Hubbard house was not a meal; it was a ceremony. Aleck used to go to it often. There at one end of the table sat Mr. Hubbard with his long shining beard and gold-rimmed spectacles. At the other end, in the bead-trimmed dress that she had worn to church, was Mrs. Hubbard, while at one side of the table were Mabel's sisters—Grace and Berta— and at the other Aleck and Mabel. There was a waitress in a fine starched apron, but she was behind a Chinese screen and sel-

79

dom came forth until the last member of
the family had laid down his fork on his
plate.

The dining room was a wonderful, sol-
emn, shining room. The walls were pan-
eled in rich red brocade, and there was an
enormous silver ice-water pitcher on the
sideboard, big enough to supply them if
they had been working all day in the
desert.

The dining room table was spread with
white linen and shining silver, and the
waitress on her expeditions from behind
the screen brought in the roast beef and
silver dishes piled high with mashed pota-
toes.

"Will you have it rare, or well done,
Mrs. Hubbard?" the host would ask his
wife politely while he sharpened his carv-
ing knife. The question was repeated to
each member of the family, although
Aleck often thought Mr. Hubbard might
have known the family tastes after so
many Sundays.

It was the same every Sunday, beginning with the soup in its gold-bordered

plates and ending with the floating island dessert with its faint flavor of bitter almonds.

One Sunday, when the ceremony of dinner was over, and Mr. and Mrs. Hubbard had gone to their rooms for a nap, and Grace and Berta had gone for a walk, Aleck and Mabel sat for a little while in the parlor. Sometimes the atmosphere of this room oppressed Aleck, with the wax flowers on the mantelpiece and the dark steel engravings on the walls. But today he did not notice the furnishings: he was too intent on what he had to tell Mabel.

"I owe the landlady three months' rent," he said. He wanted somehow to make a clean breast of his affairs. "She certainly won't let me stay there much longer if I don't pay up. . . . And the winter is coming and my coat is wearing out at the elbows. And I have to pay back Mr. Sanders, you know. He has forwarded money for our supplies. Watson hasn't had any pay for weeks. And although I've gone back to teaching the deaf, I just don't make enough with my elocution lessons. I don't want to complain, but I want you to know how it is."

"I know," Mabel said, reading his lips as clearly as if she could actually hear him speak.

"Sometimes I wonder how it will all come out," Bell continued. "How will we ever be able to marry on the amount of money I am making? How long will we have to wait?"

Mabel smiled and, leaning forward, touched his hand.

"What was the meeting you spoke to last night?" she asked.

"Oh, that," Bell answered. "That was the annual meeting of the Philosophical Society. I took the telephone there and demonstrated how it worked with drawings on a blackboard."

"Was there anyone you ever heard of in the audience?" Mabel asked.

"Oh, yes, of course," Bell answered. "There were a great many very important scientists there. I think their average age was eight-two," he said, smiling. "They all wore long black frock coats, and they all had white beards. One of them had a great big ear trumpet."

"Did you know the names of any of them?" Mabel asked.

"Of course," Bell said. "One of them was Joseph Henry—you know, the director of the Smithsonian, who was so good to me in the beginning. Another was the astronomer Simon Newcomb."

"Were they interested?" Mabel continued.

"Yes," Bell said. "They all came and shook me by the hand after I had finished speaking, and stopped to examine the instrument, and wanted to try it."

"It seems to me," Mabel said, "if those scientists at the Philosophical Society think so much of your telephone, it must be a good thing." Aleck liked to hear her call it "your telephone." He smiled, but then she said: "Why don't you take your patent papers and go and offer to sell them to the Western Union Telegraph Company? Why don't you ask for, say, a hundred thousand dollars? Then we could get married."

He looked at her in astonishment, for she had said what appeared to him an extraordinary thing. He wondered whether she had thought it out beforehand. Surely a girl with no business experience could not have been expected to make a shrewd business proposition. But that is exactly what she did.

"What an idea!" he said. And then more slowly, "What a perfectly wonderful idea."

But the wonderful idea turned out not to be so very wonderful after all. For Bell went next day with his patent papers to the Western Union Telegraph Company, was shown into the private office of a Mr. Orton, and not much more than five minutes later was shown out again, with the assurance that Western Union was not at all interested in his offer.

He went straight back to the Hubbard house after his visit to the telegraph company, for he wanted to tell Mabel what had happened. When he pulled the bell, she opened the front door herself.

"Come into the sitting room," she said.

"Mother's there. Let's tell her all about it."

Mrs. Hubbard looked up when they entered. She had been sitting near the window, reading the Boston *Transcript*. She noticed the tired expression in the young man's eyes and the taut lines around his mouth. "Come in, Aleck," she said. "Let's have a cup of tea."

"They didn't even ask me to demonstrate the telephone," he said to both of them. "You might have thought I was a crackpot with some crazy, impractical scheme in my head. They said they couldn't make use of an electrical toy."

Over the teacups and the hot buttered toast, they talked about Western Union's rejection of the telephone. "You know Mr. Hubbard doesn't get on with those telegraph people," Mrs. Hubbard said. "Maybe they have some idea that you are connected with the Hubbards." Aleck smiled, thinking that his connection so far was pretty indefinite.

She poured herself another cup of tea, making it strong, and dropped three lumps of sugar into it. "Quite against the doctor's orders," she said cheerfully, stirring the amber liquid with a thin silver spoon.

She lifted the cup halfway to her lips and then put it down on the saucer again. "I have it," she said. "I know what you could do. You could manufacture thousands of telephone instruments and sell them outright to anyone who would buy. I don't know just where you'd get the money to do it, but you'd find it somehow. Everyone would want to buy them. They could use them in offices and factories, and people giving dinner parties could telephone the invitations to their friends. Pretty soon they'd get to be the socially accepted thing. Everybody would want to buy them . . ."

"Maybe it would work," Aleck said. "I had thought of forming a company that would own the instruments and rent them. But maybe it would work to sell them outright. I could try to see about the capital . . ."

But Mrs. Hubbard's idea of manufacturing and selling the telephone instruments did not come to pass after all. While

Bell was looking around for businessmen who would supply money to manufacture the instruments, a letter was left at his room at Exeter Place that seemed to offer another source of funds. It invited Bell to address the Essex Institute of Salem at Lyceum Hall on February 12.

"If I can make a success of it, perhaps there will be other chances to lecture. Perhaps I could charge admission," he thought, and he began to consider the best way to present the telephone, not to scientists, but to the common people who might be expected to use it someday.

13
"M. H. from A. G. B."

The seats were banked in rows around the platform at Lyceum Hall in Salem so that every person in the audience had a good chance to see the stage. Light shone down from the gas jets in a large chandelier above the platform. A big black box holding the telephone instrument was placed on a table in the center of the stage. A wire stretched up from the box to the chandelier and then out through the roof, to connect with the wires of the Atlantic and Pacific Telegraph Company, and from there to the laboratory at 5 Exeter Place.

On the night of February 12 every seat

in Lyceum Hall was filled, and Alexander Graham Bell, looking very tall and slender in his Prince Albert coat, stepped up to the platform. He paused a moment, looking up at the crowded seats; then he bowed to the chairman and began to speak. His voice was very musical and clear.

"Ladies and gentlemen," he said, "I have come to show you the telephone. It is the instrument contained in this box and connected by wires with my laboratory in Boston. The principle on which it works is simple. The instrument is, indeed, much like the human ear. But the voice, instead of being carried on sound waves, travels along wires . . ."

Someone in the audience began to cough. There was a slight rustling of silken shawls.

"I do not propose to give you a detailed explanation of the telephone," he said. "That is for the scientist. I think you would prefer to have me demonstrate it to you."

There was a pause. Some of the people in the back rows stood up to see better.

Perhaps they wanted to be sure that they were not being tricked.

Then Bell leaned down, flicked a switch, and put his lips to the instrument.

"Mr. Watson," he called. "Mr. Watson, are you there? Will you speak to this audience in Salem?"

Watson was waiting in the laboratory at Exeter Place. "Ahoy! Ahoy! Mr. Bell," he shouted into the instrument.

There was a ripple of surprised laughter in the hall, and then a hushed silence.

The voice of Watson went on: "It gives me great pleasure to address you, ladies and gentlemen, although I am in Boston and you are twenty miles away in Salem." Clear and distinct, Watson's voice was carried over the wires; the people in the front rows declared afterward that they could distinguish every word.

"Will you sing for them, Mr. Watson?" Bell asked next. And Watson, his mouth close to the transmitter, sang "Hold the Fort." People said that they recognized the tune perfectly. "Sing them another song," Mr. Bell requested. And Watson obliged with "Auld Lang Syne."

The applause was uproarious. People laughed and shouted and clapped. They crowded around Bell; they wanted to hear more.

Making their way out into the quiet Salem streets when the demonstration was over, they were still filled with marvel and excitement, for they had heard an incredible thing, a voice that had come all the way from Boston to Salem.

Two days later Bell received a letter bearing a Salem postmark. He opened it and read:

PROF. A. GRAHAM BELL

Dear Sir—

A general desire has been expressed among our citizens that you should repeat the very interesting and instructive lecture of Monday evening last on Telephony, and we shall be pleased if your occupations will allow you to comply with this invitation, to devote another evening in Salem to experiments with the telephone, at such time as you may designate.

The letter was signed by sixteen of the

leading citizens of Salem.

So about a week later the experiments in "Telephony" were repeated. This time the audience numbered five hundred, and the program was a little longer and more elaborate. A Salem minister came to the platform and, putting his mouth down to the transmitter, inquired whether it was raining in Boston. Mr. Watson informed him that it was not. Another leading citizen was invited to speak over the telephone and inquired about the strike of the engineers on the Boston and Maine Railroad. He was informed that the trains were running. Then Bell invited the Reverend E. C. Bolles to take the transmitter, and that gentleman declared ceremoniously, "I shake hands with you cordially in imagination twenty miles away."

After that Watson sang "Hold the Fort" again, and again people recognized the tune and marveled.

The second demonstration in Salem was a huge success. Best of all, it netted eighty-five dollars in gate receipts. Aleck carried the money back to Boston in his pocket, filled with plans of what he would do with it. He would now be able to pay his landlady. He would use some of it to pay Mr. Sanders, who had helped him so generously. Some of it must surely go to Mr. Watson. Eighty-five dollars was not really very much. Still, there would be other lectures, he was sure. The audience had seemed so excited. If he could get other lectures, enough of them, surely the day was not far off when he could marry Mabel.

He arrived in the deserted Boston station and made his way through the dark Boston streets to Exeter Place. There, during the night, another plan—a more important plan for the use of the money—came into his mind.

Next day, the eighty-five dollars still in his pocket, Bell went down the three flights of stairs to the street and walked briskly along until he came to a small silversmith's shop. A bell jangled as he pushed open the door, and a white-haired silversmith in a leather apron put down his work and rose to meet him.

"Good afternoon, sir," he said politely. "Is there anything I can do for you?"

"Yes," Bell answered. "I want to get a miniature model made, a replica of the telephone. I want it made of pure silver."

"I'm afraid I don't know exactly what that would be like," the silversmith answered. "I have heard of a telephone, but I have never seen one, or a picture of one, even."

"It would be like this," Bell answered. "Have you a piece of paper and a pencil?"

Then, while the silversmith watched, he sketched carefully, in full detail, the instrument over which he had worked so many months.

Bell's pencil paused at last. "Do you understand?" he asked. "Do you think that you could make it?"

The silversmith took up the sketch and held it out before him, studying it. "Yes," he said at last. "I think I understand."

"Do you think you could make it in silver, only much smaller?" Bell asked.

"Of course I could," the silversmith answered. "But it would be expensive, very expensive."

"How much would it cost?" Bell asked.

The silversmith took the pencil and began to figure, stopping now and again to rub his ear and then going on with his calculations. At length he had finished.

"It would cost ninety dollars," he said.

"Could you possibly make it for eighty-five?" Bell asked.

The silversmith paused and rubbed his ear again. "Yes," he said. "I think I could."

"Then make it," Bell said. "And the sooner the better. If I could have it tomorrow . . ."

"Tomorrow?" the silversmith said. "Yes, I think I could have it tomorrow."

"Good," said Bell, and he turned to go. But then he turned again. "Could you engrave some letters on it?" he asked. "Could you mark it *M. H. from A. G. B.?* And the date?"

The silversmith smiled. "Yes," he said. "I think I could do that too, without any extra charge."

14

"It's Time
You Married"

Gardiner Greene Hubbard left his law office early that April afternoon in 1877. His coach stood outside at the curb with its dappled horses and its uniformed driver on the box. The coachman jumped down at Mr. Hubbard's approach to open the door for him.

"I'm going straight home this afternoon, John," Mr. Hubbard said. "I won't want to stop at the club."

They started at a smart trot along the crowded Boston streets, and Mr. Hubbard sat back comfortably against the cushions, turning his business affairs over in his mind. Riding to and from his office was the best opportunity he had for reflection, he used to say. No one came in to interrupt him in his coach.

He was glad, now that he took time to think about it, that he had put money into mining stock. The mines of the West were certainly producing more than anyone had dared to hope. And the railroads were doing well too, now that they had finally got established. Crowds of people were moving west now. Every day the ships were bringing thousands of immigrants bound for the new lands beyond the mountains.

Idly his mind began to picture the farms, the ranches, the new towns. There was room for thousands and thousands of people out there. And where the people were, there were expanding markets and opportunities for business.

"What this country needs, of course, is to be bound more closely together," he thought. "The people must have some

way of keeping in touch with each other:
loneliness is one of the greatest difficulties
the new settlers have to fight. And they'll
have to have some way of keeping in touch
with the East, and with the government in
Washington."

As he thought about it he was glad that
he had joined with George Sanders, the
leather manufacturer, and with young
Aleck Bell in backing the harmonic telegraph. That might speed up communication, if it could be worked out.

And now here was young Bell's other
invention, the telephone. He had not
thought much of it at first: he had urged
Bell to stick to the telegraph. But Bell had
worked on it anyhow—the young blighter.
And he was doing pretty well with it
too—that award at the Centennial, and the
lectures in Salem. Recently he had been
invited to lecture in New York, and Watson had talked from New York to New
Brunswick. Maybe the idea would come to
something. Mrs. Hubbard seemed to think
a good deal of young Bell. And Mabel, of

course . . . Perhaps it would be wise to back the telephone after all.

"Here we are, sir." The coach had drawn up at the door of his house, and the driver was holding the door open for him.

"Good night, John," he said as he got out and began to climb up the steps.

"Mrs. Hubbard and Miss Mabel have gone out, sir." The elderly maid in her starched apron and ruffled cap opened the front door for him.

Mr. Hubbard handed her his hat and gloves. "Thank you, Margaret," he said. "Will you bring me some coffee in the library?"

In a comfortable chair near the window, Mr. Hubbard sat, sipping his coffee. Some wrens were building a nest in the branch of a tree outside. They made a great chatter and fuss as they worked, but Mr. Hubbard did not hear them; he was reading the stock-market quotations.

So absorbed was he that young Aleck Bell had to knock twice at the library door before Mr. Hubbard knew that he was there. Finally he heard him and looked up.

"Come in," he called.

Aleck opened the door and stood looking for a moment at the older man.

"Glad to see you, Aleck," Mr. Hubbard said kindly. "Sit down, won't you? Have some coffee."

Without waiting for an answer to his invitation, Mr. Hubbard rose and, taking up the silver coffeepot that stood on the tray on his desk, poured the coffee carefully, watching the dark liquid fill the little cup in his hand. He passed it to the young man.

"How are things going?" he asked, settling into his chair again. "I hear that your demonstrations have been a great success."

"They've gone pretty well, I think," Aleck said. There was a pause.

"And what's the next step?" Mr. Hubbard asked, raising his cup to enjoy the fragrance of the dark liquid it held.

"Colonel Reynolds of Providence, you know, wants to form an English company," Aleck said. "They want me to go to England with the telephone."

"Splendid!" Mr. Hubbard responded. "We'll need more telephones in America than anywhere else, of course, but still if they want to install a system in England— Why, what's the matter, man? You might think that someone had suggested that you rob your grandmother!"

It was true. Aleck sat, his coffee cup in his hand, and on his pale face was a look of utter misery.

"England is a long way off," he said at last. "It takes fourteen days just to get there."

"Of course it does." Mr. Hubbard looked at him in astonishment. "I've been there several times. The ships don't sink."

But Aleck did not smile.

"Mabel and I want to get married," he said. "I don't want to go there by myself."

Mr. Hubbard's face softened.

"You've been engaged some time," he said. "How long is it now?"

"Two years," Aleck answered, as if he were speaking of the cosmic ages.

"Two years is long enough," Mr. Hubbard answered. "It's time you married. I could advance some of the money I planned to invest in the telephone. Perhaps that would be a good way to invest it. You might take her to England on your wedding trip. . . . Here, let me fill your cup again."

15

A Wedding Present for the Bride

That summer the Hubbard house on Brattle Street was filled with preparations. There was hardly a quiet corner to be found in it. In one room the seamstresses sat sewing in drifts of muslin, linen, and taffeta. Mabel was in constant demand to have a blouse fitted, a skirt hung, a little straw hat tried on. In another room three patient women sat addressing envelopes:

Mr. and Mrs. Gardiner Greene Hubbard
announce the marriage
of their daughter Mabel . . .

Up and down the steps the messenger boys were running with packages. Now it was a large gilt clock from the Hubbards' cousin in New York; now a set of dishes, hand-painted; now a lamp with a round, hand-painted glass shade; now a mirror. And there were countless other things to be unwrapped, listed, and acknowledged with a note from the bride. Mrs. Hubbard directed all these activities with a competent hand. But Aleck and Mabel watched the preparations and wondered that there should be such pomp and glitter just because they were going to marry each other.

After a time the seamstresses and secretaries gave way to the florist and caterers, and still the parade of delivery boys continued to bring their packages.

"So many people have given you gifts, Mabel," Aleck said the afternoon before their wedding. "I want to give you one too. I have it here."

They were sitting in the garden behind the house, for all the rooms downstairs had been emptied of furniture in preparation for the next day's crowds. Now Aleck drew a long white envelope from his pocket, looked at it a moment, and handed it to her. "Miss Mabel Hubbard," he had written carefully on the envelope.

"It's all legal," he said. "I saw the law-yers yesterday."

Mabel tore open the envelope, drew out a large sheet of paper, and read:

"I, Alexander Graham Bell, do hereby give to Mabel Hubbard, my future wife, all moneys and all interests which may come to me by reason of the invention of the telephone. Any stocks which I hold either here or abroad, shall be transferred to her name—"

She stopped reading. "Oh, Aleck," she said. "You are giving me all your future."

"That's what I want to do," he said.

"How do you know I shall be able to take care of it?"

She held the paper in her hand as if it were a string of rubies and diamonds.

"It's not a great gift yet," he said. "Per-haps someday it may be."

The wedding was to be at noon, July 11,

1877. Aleck reached the Hubbard house early and stood waiting in an upstairs room. He was very slender in his new dark suit, and his face was a little paler than it usually was. Somewhere in the big house Mabel was getting ready. He thought of the white dress that he had not yet seen, the filmy veil. He wished that his mother and father could have been there with him that day. But the distance from Ontario to Boston was much too great to make that possible. Anyway, he and Mabel would go to Ontario to see them. That would be the first journey of their married life.

He walked to a window and drew aside the curtain to look down at the throng of people coming up the steps. As the carriages came rolling along the drive Aleck was aware of the swish of silk dresses, the odor of perfume, though he was not actually near enough to sense either one. He watched for some time, and then his attention was drawn to two men who were walking through the gate.

"It's Watson," he said to himself. "Watson and Eddy Wilson from Williams' shop. They must have come all the way in the horsecars!"

As he watched, the two men drew aside from the throng and walked across the lawn to a large syringa bush. The shrubbery hid them from the wedding guests, but Aleck, standing in the window, saw them plainly.

From their pockets he saw each man draw a brand-new pair of white gloves, crumple up the paper in which they were wrapped, and put it back in his pocket. Then carefully they drew the gloves over their hands, fastened the buttons, stood for a brief moment hesitant, and squaring their shoulders walked across the grass and up the steps with the other guests.

"Dear old Watson," Bell said to himself with a rush of feeling. "Eddy Wilson too. They've come to my wedding. And they've brought white gloves. I don't believe either one of them ever had a pair of white gloves in his life before. . . ."

He felt content to think that those hands, so competent in winding coils and working with electromagnets, should now be wearing white gloves for his sake.

"It's time to start, Aleck." Mr. Hubbard had entered the room behind him. The music of the wedding march was drifting up the stairs.

16

Conversation
on Shipboard

The S.S. *Anchoria* made its way across the North Atlantic toward Scotland. The ocean had been very rough, but today it was smooth again; the fog hung close down over the surface of the sea. The great foghorn blew with a steady rhythm, so regular that the passengers took it for granted, like the throb of the ship's engine.

Aleck and Mabel had put their deck chairs on the lee side of the vessel and had wrapped themselves warmly in steamer rugs.

"The captain says we'll be within sight of land tomorrow morning," Aleck said. "Ailsa Craig—it's the first bit of Scotland. Even if you're sound asleep I'll wake you up to see it."

"You're more likely to be asleep yourself," Mabel answered. "Haven't I been up first every morning since we started?"

Aleck smiled. The sea air certainly made her eyes extraordinarily bright and her cheeks extraordinarily pink, he thought.

"I think you'll like Scotland," he said. "The heather and the bleak, rocky land. They'll give us kippers for breakfast, and porridge, and tea so strong you can hardly put your spoon into it."

Mabel laughed. "Your mother's tea is pretty strong."

Aleck's face softened at the mention of his mother. "You liked her, didn't you?" he said.

"I liked your mother and your father too," she answered. "Do you remember how your father jumped out of the surrey when he met us at the station, and how hard he kissed me, because I was your wife?"

"Yes," Aleck said. "And do you remember how Mother came running out of the house when we got home, and the great big oatcake she broke over your head? I can still see the surprised look you had at that greeting. . . . You didn't know a bride would never go hungry in her husband's house if the oatcake was broken over her head, did you?"

They both laughed. It seemed to them that there was something very sweet in Mrs. Bell's observance of the old Scottish custom.

"I hope you never *will* be hungry," Aleck said then, looking at her somewhat doubtfully. Certainly she seemed extremely well nourished now, with her full red lips and her hair tucked neatly under her soft fur hat.

"It seems to me that the telephone may do well for us," he said. "I can imagine that some time in the future—not yet, of course—a great many people might want to have telephones. Maybe it would be possible to have not only a single telephone line, like the one Charles Williams has between his house and his office, but a good many lines that meet together in one central place. Then you could call a central operator and tell him what person you wanted to talk to, and the operator could make a connection, and you could talk to that person, if he had a telephone."

"How would he know you wanted to talk to him? He couldn't sit there with the receiver at his ear, waiting."

"No," Aleck answered. "He couldn't do that. But I should think it could be fixed so there was a click or a buzz or something to attract his attention. I don't think that would be very hard to do."

"And then I thought of another thing," Mabel went on. "Suppose somebody in my family was sick and I wanted to call a doctor. Instead of running to the doctor's office, I might call on the telephone."

"Yes," Aleck said. "I should think you could."

"But how would I know whether that particular doctor had a telephone? Maybe he'd be one of the people who didn't."

"I thought of that too," Aleck said. "I think we'd have to make a book with the names of all the people who had sub-scribed to the telephone. Every person who subscribed would have one of these books. Then if you wanted to call your doctor, you could just look and see. . . ."

So they sat planning and dreaming of a world that would be a different one be-cause of the invention that Aleck had made. Neither of them could quite imag-ine what it would be like, for even they could not tell what the future held.

For a long time they sat, wrapped in their steamer rugs, with the fog blowing around them. People came and went, pac-ing around the deck. Now and again the wet spray flew up over the rail and splashed on the deck before them. And still they talked on, trying to imagine how their invention could be adapted for peo-ple's use.

After a long time a steward in a white coat walked by them beating a big brass gong.

"It's dinnertime," Aleck said, throwing back his rug. "Let's go down."

17
The House
in Kensington

They stayed two weeks in the fishing village on the Scottish coast, and then they went to London.

"We'll get a house," Aleck said, remembering the comfortable house his grandfather had lived in. "You'll be the mistress of the house and entertain the people who come there. I'll lecture about the telephone. Colonel Reynolds has probably made some lecture engagements already. He said he would."

That was in fact the way it turned out.

Colonel Reynolds was a businessman interested in introducing the telephone in England, and he had arranged a series of lectures for the inventor.

The house that the Bells rented was a large, comfortable one in Kensington, with lace curtains at every window. Long pier glasses in gilded frames reflected Mabel's silken ruffles and the light on her curly brown hair. There were glowing coal fires in the grates, and china cups thin as eggshells into which she poured the tea for visitors.

Sometimes, late in the afternoon when the lamps were lighted and the guests lingered on, the talk would turn to the telephone.

"We've run a wire into the back parlor," Aleck would say. "If you want to hear it, go in there. Hold the tube up close to your ear."

And while the guests in the back parlor took turns holding the telephone to their ears, Aleck would sit down at the piano and begin to play.

"Gin a body meet a body"—the melody

would float softly through the room while his fingers moved across the keys— "comin' through the rye."

But before long his playing would be interrupted. The guests would come rushing back into the drawing room. "We heard it quite plainly," they would exclaim. "Every note of it! Every single note! It's the most extraordinary thing! Play it again."

And Aleck would say, "Go back into the other room again. Don't forget to hold the tube close to your ear." And he would start to play again, thinking how pleasant it was to have the drawing room quiet and the door closed.

But all their time was not spent in entertaining, for they had come to England to interest British investors in forming an English telephone company. Mabel worked as hard as Aleck in getting the idea of the telephone across to the British public. From the very beginning she took care of his correspondence, reading, answering, and filing the letters that arrived in larger and larger numbers. When technical replies were necessary, she took them down from Aleck's dictation, reading his lips with unfailing accuracy.

"The Society of Arts is writing to ask you to repeat the lecture you gave them," she said one morning, looking up from a desk covered with papers. "They say that hundreds of people were not able to get into the hall when you talked to them. Anyone who has already heard your lecture will not be permitted to come again."

Aleck smiled. It seemed to him rather absurd that anyone should want to come to hear the same thing twice, even if it was about the telephone.

"Look at this, Aleck," Mabel said another day. "They want you to show the telephone at the Crystal Palace on Boxing Day. They seem to think there may be as many as fifty thousand people there."

One morning an impressive invitation came from the Society of Telegraph Engineers in London. Later there was a request to Professor Bell to deliver a series of lectures at Oxford University on his method of teaching the deaf.

With energy born of enthusiasm for their invention, Mabel and Aleck both worked. Aleck met his schedule of lectures, and the attendance at them grew.

In the meantime, the newspapers began to write articles about the changed world that the telephone would bring about. *Punch*, the English magazine, printed a set of New Year's resolutions that included:

> To make an effort to get up earlier in the morning.
>
> To make myself thoroughly acquainted with the Eastern Question in all its bearings, the relations between Capital and Labour, the principle and construction of the telephone . . .

It was after that that the capitalists, riding on the tide of popular approval, began to talk of organizing the English company for which the Bells had hoped.

"They want me to write a prospectus," Aleck told Mabel one day. "They want to know how we think the telephone could be used in business."

Mabel's mind went back to the S.S. *Anchoria*, to the afternoon that they had sat together on the deck. "You won't have any difficulty in doing that," she said.

"I don't suppose I will," Aleck answered. "I'll write out a rough draft tonight before I go to bed. Then maybe you could polish it off tomorrow—all the spelling and punctuation and everything, and see if I have said it the right way. And copy it in that neat businesslike hand of yours. You know."

"Yes," Mabel said. "I know."

That night, after Mabel had gone to bed, Aleck sat writing. This is what he wrote:

"To the Capitalists of the Electric Telephone Company." He paused and sat looking into the fire for a few minutes, then he wrote again:

At the present time we have a perfect network of gas-pipes and water-pipes through our large cities. We have main pipes laid under the streets communicating by side pipes with the various dwellings, enabling the members to draw their supplies of gas and water from a common source.

In a similar manner, it is conceivable that cables of telephone wires could be laid underground, or suspended overhead, commu-

nicating by branch wires with private dwellings, counting houses, shops, manufactories,
etc., etc., uniting them through the main
cable with a central office where the wires
could be connected as desired, establishing
direct communication between any two
places in the city. Such a plan as this, though
impracticable at the present moment, will, I
firmly believe, be the outcome of the intro-
duction of the telephone to the public. Not
only so, but I believe in the future, wires will
unite the head offices of the Telephone Company in different cities, and a man in one part
of the country may communicate by word of
mouth with another in a distant place.

He paused and put down his pen. What
he had written seemed extraordinarily
bold to him. He read it through a second
time. He was sure that every word he had
written would certainly come to pass.

He rose and, taking up the paper, laid it
carefully on Mabel's desk. Then, cupping
his hand around the top of the chimney, he
blew out the lamp and went upstairs.

18
An Audience
with the Queen

The command to exhibit the telephone to Queen Victoria came in a white envelope so large as to make all the rest of the morning mail seem unimportant. Mabel slit it open with her paper-knife and drew the letter out.

"It's from the Queen's secretary," she said. "They want you to bring the telephone to the Palace at Osborne and show it to Queen Victoria."

She held the letter out for Aleck to see—the gilded coat-of-arms, the careful script, the flourishes of the secretary's signature.

"Osborne is way off on the Isle of Wight, isn't it?" said Aleck. "I'd have to take the railway down to Portsmouth, and then the steamer. It would take ages to get there, and more ages to get back again. And I have so many engagements here in London."

"What does that matter?" Mabel answered.

The visit to the Queen had been arranged by Kate Field, an American singer who had agreed to act as Bell's press agent. Such a visit could not be undertaken without a good deal of planning on Aleck's part too. He visited the tailor for a new dark suit, and the bootmaker and the hatter for shoes and a hat. At Mabel's suggestion he sought out a gentleman acquainted with court etiquette and found out that he must never presume to speak directly to the monarch, but that she must be addressed through a third person.

Finally he planned the program. He thought there should be music of a rather elegant nature, since it was to be heard by royal ears, and he decided to invite Kate Field to perform. She was then very popular in London. Miss Field bought a new blue silk dress sprigged with rosebuds, in the hope that she might be presented to the Queen. But in this she was disappointed.

It was on January 11, 1877, that the smoky little locomotive pulled and jerked their railway carriage out of the London station. There were four of them: Miss Field with a maid; Colonel Ponsonby, who was organizing the English telephone company; and Aleck. Their train went jerking along toward the south, the telephone, carefully wrapped in its box, lying on the seat of the railway carriage.

At Portsmouth they changed to a brightly painted little steamer, and so crossed the Solent Water and were at last in the harbor at Spithead. There the carriage from the Palace was waiting to meet them.

They climbed into it, and the horses started up the road at a smart trot. And soon they had left the sea behind them and were rolling along under winter branches toward the rambling, ornate house that Albert and Victoria had built as a home for their growing family.

It took only a short time to connect the telephone wires between the Palace and Osborne Cottage, where the Queen's secretary lived. From the cottage, the line extended to the town of Cowes. Telegraph wires already connected Cowes, Southampton, and London, and arrangements had been made to use them for the demonstration. At last the instruments were put in place and tested, and everything was ready.

Then Miss Field and Colonel Ponsonby retired to Osborne Cottage to await the hour of the demonstration, and Aleck was given his dinner in a small sitting room of the Palace. The roast beef and Yorkshire pudding and stewed figs were exactly what might have been served at his mother's house, he thought.

Dinner over, he sat waiting, some notes that he had written in his hand. It was very cold in the room, for Queen Victoria would not tolerate wasting fuel by heating any of her apartments more than was necessary.

"But I should think a fire *is* necessary in January," Aleck said to himself. And then he smiled. "Mabel would probably say that I'm cold because I'm nervous," he thought. "Maybe she'd be right."

He fell to thinking about how the demonstration would go. Would it be hard to explain a telephone to a queen, he wondered. He had demonstrated it to a great many people, and they had understood at least the basics of its working. Would Queen Victoria follow his explanations? She understood the intricacies of domestic and foreign politics, but whether she had any basis for understanding scientific theories he had no idea. He must make it quite simple and clear.

There was a knock at the door, and a white-haired servant entered.

"It is nine o'clock, Mr. Bell," he said. "Will you come in?"

Once more, as he entered Queen Victoria's council room, Aleck was reminded of his mother's house. The carpet was patterned with roses, and long lace curtains hung from the windows. A gilded clock ticked on the mantelpiece and an oil lamp burned on the table, for though gaslights were burning in the great houses of London then, something so new as gaslights had not been brought to Osborne.

A number of people were seated on small gilt chairs around the council room, and the usher led Aleck from one of them to another. "Princess Beatrice." "The Honorable Mrs. Ponsonby." "The Duke of Connaught."

To each in turn Aleck made a deep bow, and the members of the Royal Household observed that the young inventor's dark sideburns and pale cheeks lent him a certain air of distinction.

He had hardly reached the table where the telephone was installed when the door opened again and the Queen entered. Briskly, her silken skirts rustling softly, she walked across the council chamber, nodding to the members of the Royal

Household. Then she seated herself in a low chair near the place where Bell stood.

"She looks exactly like her pictures," he was thinking. His eyes moved from her frilled white cap to the rich pearls that hung in strings around her neck, the jewels that gleamed from the brooch on her breast, the plump arms that seemed to him a little red and chapped.

"It is the young American inventor, Mr. Alexander Graham Bell," the usher was saying. "He has come to demonstrate the telephone to Your Majesty."

The Queen nodded. The proceedings had begun.

Explaining the principles on which the telephone worked was such a familiar thing that Aleck forgot his nervousness. How many times before had he told of the undulating current, of the little diaphragm that acted like an eardrum? He spoke clearly and simply, his melodious voice filling the room as it had so often filled larger chambers than this.

The members of the Royal Household were quiet, listening. The Queen with her pearls and her black silk ruffles seemed unmoved. Aleck had no way of knowing whether she had followed what he said or not.

Finally his talk was ended. "I should like to give you an actual demonstration now," he said. "This instrument has been connected with Osborne Cottage. If Her Majesty will hold the tube to her ear, it should be possible for her to hear Miss Field, who is stationed there."

The Duke of Connaught stepped forward. He took the telephone from Aleck and offered it to the Queen. Aleck saw her take it, and then he leaned down to turn the switch that started the current. But when he looked up again, he saw that the Queen had turned completely around to talk to Princess Beatrice, who was seated behind her.

"Listen, Your Majesty," Aleck said in consternation. He knew Miss Field must already have begun to sing. Queen Victoria would miss half of "Kathleen Mavourneen." "Put the tube up to your ear," he said, and he gave her shoulder a little push to attract attention.

He had no sooner touched the silk-clad shoulder than he realized that he had made a breach of etiquette. It was considered wrong even to speak directly to the Queen, and he had actually pushed her shoulder. The people in the room seemed to freeze in disapproval. "A young man from America," their faces said.

But the Queen turned with great dignity, and without comment took up the tube and placed it to the ear where a ruby and diamond pendant hung. Then her face broke into a smile. "Kathleen Mavourneen," she murmured.

"Miss Field is singing now," Aleck said to the people in the council room. "When the music is finished, we shall try to establish communication with Cowes, Southampton, and finally London. . . ."

❧

"How did it go?" Mabel asked him when he reached home. "Was the Queen interested?"

"I don't know, really," he replied.

Not many days later the question was answered. Once again a letter with the royal coat-of-arms arrived in the mail, and Aleck and Mabel, looking at it together, read:

My dear sir:

I hope you are aware how much gratified and surprised the Queen was at the exhibition of the telephone here on Monday evening.

Her Majesty desires me to express her thanks to you and the ladies and gentlemen who were associated with you on that occasion.

The Queen would like, if there is no reason against it, to purchase the two instruments which are still here, with the wires attached. Perhaps you would be so kind as to let me know to whom the sum due should be paid.

I am, dear sir, very faithfully yours,

Thomas Biddulph

"So she did like it," Mabel said.

19
Threat of Disaster

Aleck wrote to America and asked Mr. Watson to make a pair of ivory telephones for the Queen. But before they could be finished, she had lost interest and would not accept them. That did not greatly matter to Aleck and Mabel, for at about that time their first child was born in the house in Kensington—a first baby makes other matters seem unimportant.

Not long after, though, they were jerked back to reality. A message came from Thomas Watson. There was trouble with the patent for the telephone.

During the eighteen months that the Bells had spent in England, telephone wires had been strung from place to place in America with surprising speed. Mr. Hubbard had organized the telephone company's business affairs. Mr. Sanders had put thousands of dollars into it. Thomas Watson, somewhat fearfully, had resigned from Williams' shop to help.

More and more people were becoming interested in the new invention. Businessmen, feeling very adventurous and modern, were installing telephones in their offices. Families had the clumsy looking boxes attached to their parlor walls. Doctors and lawyers considered the wisdom of using them for convenience in talking to their clients. The telephone linesmen were busy, and poles were rising in the streets like the trees of a fast-growing forest.

Mr. Sanders and Mr. Hubbard began to feel that their money had been wisely invested. Mr. Watson ceased to regret that he had given up the chance to be a fore-man. The new company that Aleck had given to Mabel Bell for a wedding present appeared to be making her a fortune.

And then catastrophe, like a black cloud, threatened them all. For the Western Union Telegraph Company began manu-facturing and distributing telephones of its own. Bell had no right to his patent, they said. Their men had thought of making telephones long before Bell ever did. They would prove it in the courts.

"Have you any papers, and diaries or letters written at the time you were work-ing on the telephone—anything to prove when you made it?" Mr. Watson wrote to Bell in England.

Bell shook his head when he read the letter. "I've never been systematic about such things," he said. "I'll have to tell him I didn't save anything like that at all. I lent Kate Field the only notebook I had, and she lost it."

But the next ship from America brought a more reassuring message. "I have searched the rooms at Exeter Place thoroughly," Mr. Watson wrote. "They had not been cleaned since we left them, and I found a scrap basket which had never been emptied. In it was the first sketch you made of the telephone, and this will be valuable evidence. But you must come home at once. It is imperative that you come and defend the patent in the Circuit Court."

They sailed for home in October 1878. And all the while Aleck grew more and more angry.

"I won't have anything more to do with the telephone," he said. "What good has it ever done us? I refuse to take part in bickerings and quarrelings. Defend my case indeed! I can go back to teaching. That's useful work. You and the baby can stay with my mother and father until I find a position. Then we can be together again."

Mabel said nothing, waiting to see how things would turn out.

They had been in Canada only a day or two when Watson arrived.

"I didn't send a message," he said. "I didn't think it would do any good. I thought you wouldn't come—and you've got to. I'm here to bring you back to Boston. You must file a statement so that the telephone company can complete its evidence in the case."

"I won't do any such thing," Bell answered.

"But you'll have to," Watson said quietly. "It wouldn't be right to let those people run off with your patent. It wouldn't be just or fair. There isn't only one person now who claims to have invented the telephone—there are five! You've got to start for Boston tomorrow. It's a matter of justice."

Bell smiled. Watson never mentioned the hours of work he himself had put into the invention, or the fact that he had risked his future to get it established. Nor did he mention that Mr. Sanders had invested all the capital he had earned in a long business career, or the fact that Mr. Hubbard had contributed all his organizing skill to getting the telephone company established. He simply talked of justice.

"All right," Bell said at last. "I've just unpacked my bag, but I can pack it up again. Mabel and the baby had better stay on here awhile."

20
A Legal Statement Is Filed

It was good to be with Watson on the long journey from Quebec to Boston. The two friends sat close together on the red plush seat and talked hour after hour.

"People are really beginning to believe in the telephone," Watson told him. "They don't consider it a toy anymore. They are beginning to think it will be indispensable to business. They talk of how quickly they can get fire engines or doctors or even policemen by using it. Mr. Hubbard believes that our telephone company will be a great business. He even believes Mr. Sanders will recover all the thousands of dollars he has put into it. And now Western Union wants to start manufacturing telephones of its own! It hasn't any right to, of course. But its lawyers claim that your patent is worthless."

Bell looked amused. It had not been very long since he had offered to sell the invention to Western Union, and Mr. Orton had told him they could not use "an electrical toy."

"It's true," he said. "Other men have dreamed of sending speech along a wire. The only difference is that none of them has ever done it."

The rattling train went swaying southward. White farmhouses, rocky fields, and herds of cattle flashed past the car windows. Here the train crossed a river over a high trestle; there it slowed down to pass through a town with its locomotive panting and its whistle screeching.

After a while darkness fell outside.

There were lights in the farmhouses. A trainman came through the car to light the swaying lamps.

In the light of the hanging lamps Watson noticed that Bell had grown deathly pale.

"Are you all right?" he asked.

"Could I put my head down there on the seat?" Bell answered. "It seems to be aching so."

Quickly Watson took off his coat and rolled it up for a pillow. By the time he had lifted Bell and put his head down, the inventor had lost consciousness.

Watson took him immediately to Massachusetts General Hospital when they reached Boston, and once again, as he had done in the rooms at Exeter Place, he watched Bell fight his way back to recovery. But this time Bell's bed was not under an attic roof. It was in a clean, comfortable hospital room. And this time he had skilled, trained nurses to take care of him.

The last day for filing the statement that would complete the evidence in defending the patent in the telephone case was No-

vember 20, 1878. Watson watched Bell
lying sick and listless in his hospital bed
and wondered whether all the work that
they had done together would come to
nothing after all. If the legal evidence was
not filed, their case would certainly be lost.

But rest and quiet and good nourish-
ment did their work for Aleck as they had
done before. One morning he was able to
sit up, propped against pillows, for a little
while, and then he was asking his nurse for
pencil and paper, and then he was writing.
Clear, brief, conclusive, the words followed each other—the statement of what
he had done and how he had done it. Tired
at last, he put down his pencil, then took it
up again to sign his name: "A. Graham
Bell."

"I'll take it to the lawyer at once," Watson said. He had been sitting in a chair beside the bed while Aleck wrote.

They waited impatiently to hear the
court's verdict on November 20. But before the court convened, a message came
from the lawyer. He had shown Aleck's
statement to Western Union, and they had

decided to withdraw the case.

A little weak and tired, but happy, Aleck rose from his bed and dressed. Watson went with him to the railroad station, where he took the train back to Canada.

21
"Ahoy! Ahoy! Mr. Bell"

That was not the only lawsuit that threatened Bell. Six hundred suits were brought against him by jealous inventors who hoped to get some of the rich profits away from Bell Telephone Associates.

Aleck found himself so busy preparing for the suits that he and Mabel bought a house in Washington to be nearer the Supreme Court. He had to stop everything else and devote himself entirely to defending patent cases. But it was worthwhile, for every verdict was in his favor.

In the meantime, others continued to work at what he had begun. In 1877 Gardiner Greene Hubbard and Thomas A. Watson had sent out the first advertisement. It was modestly worded as follows:

> The proprietors of the Telephone, the invention of Alexander Graham Bell, for which patents have been issued in the United States and Great Britain, are now prepared to furnish Telephones for the transmission of articulate speech through instruments not more than twenty miles apart. Conversation can be easily carried on after slight practice and with the occasional repetition of a word or sentence. On first listening to the Telephone, though the sound is perfectly audible, the articulation seems to be indistinct but after a few trials the ear becomes accustomed to the peculiar sound and finds little difficulty in understanding the words.
>
> The Telephone should be set in a quiet place where there is no noise which would intercept ordinary conversation.
>
> The advantages of the Telephone over the telegraph for local conversation are:
>
> 1st, that no skilled operator is required but direct communication may be had by speech without requiring the intervention of a third person.

2nd, that the communication is much more rapid, the average number of words transmitted by Morse Sounder being from fifteen to twenty, by Telephone from one to two hundred.

3rd, that no expense is required either for its operation, maintenance, or repair.

The terms for leasing two Telephones for social purposes connecting a dwelling house with any other building will be $20. a year, for business purposes $40. a year, payable semi-annually in advance, with the cost of expressage from New York, Boston, Cincinnati, Chicago, St. Louis, or San Francisco. The instrument will be kept in good working order by the lessors, free of expense except from injuries resulting from great carelessness.

Several Telephones can be placed on the same line at an additional rental of $10. for each instrument; but the use of more than two on the same line where privacy is required, is not advised. Any person within ordinary hearing distance can hear the voice calling through the Telephone. If a louder call is required one can be furnished for $5.

Telephone lines will be constructed by the proprietors if desired. The price will vary from $100. to $150. a mile; any good mechanic can construct a line; No. 9 wire costs 8½ cents a pound, 220 pounds to the mile; 34

insulators at 25 cents each; the price of poles and setting varies in every locality; stringing wire $5. a mile; sundries $10. a mile.

Parties leasing the Telephone incur no expense beyond the annual rental and the repair of the line wire.

On the following page are extracts from the press and other sources concerning the Telephone.

Gardiner G. Hubbard

For further information—Thos. A. Watson
                             10A Court Street
                             Boston

The response to the advertisement seemed amazing. People everywhere began to think that they must have telephones installed. Businessmen began to consider themselves old-fashioned unless they did business over the telephone. Families began to depend on telephones for making their social engagements. People talked of how much safer they felt if they could call the police or the fire department quickly. And all this meant that more and more poles were set in place every day, and miles and miles of copper wire were strung across the sky.

Alexander Graham Bell watched the speed of the telephone's growth with amazement. Although he had always believed that the telephone would have a great future, he had no way of knowing that its growth would be so rapid.

In 1877 an experimental telephone switchboard was put in service in Boston with boys as operators. But girls proved to be quicker and more skilled in making connections, and they soon replaced the boys in the central offices.

As the number of subscribers grew directories were printed, as Aleck Bell had guessed. The first of these, published in New Haven, Connecticut, about a month after the exchange opened there, had eight names. But it was very quickly replaced by another. This directory listed eleven homes, three doctors, two dentists, twenty stores and factories, four meat and fish markets, two horsecab and boarding stables. There were also eight other subscribers, among them the police department and the post office.

And all the while the service on the

telephone grew more efficient. The "thumper" that Watson had invented to attract the attention of the person being called was followed by a buzzer, and the buzzer was replaced by a bell. The old handle that you ground to attract the attention of the operator at the central office was replaced by a hook that rang the operator automatically when you lifted the receiver from it. The old greeting "Ahoy!" was replaced by the more modern "Hello!"

After a while the network of copper wires spread so thick above the city streets that it was decided to run them underground along with the water pipes, gas pipes, and electric-light wires. But in country places the wires still stretched from pole to pole, and linesmen braved all kinds of weather to keep them in repair.

So, as the years passed, the telephone lines went stretching farther and farther out across the country. Night and day they carried their messages—messages of business, of politics, of love, birth, and death—until the network spread from

New York to Chicago and on out farther west than that.

By 1915 they stretched all the way across the continent. There was a great celebration that day, January 25 it was, when the connection was joined between the East and West coasts. No less a person than the President of the United States took part in the opening ceremony.

That day, at his desk in the White House, Woodrow Wilson held the receiver to his ear and listened. There was a crackling sound, a pause, and then, clear and plain, the voice of the governor of California. The thin, austere face of the President broke into a smile. In his imagination he saw the mountains and the wide plains. And in his imagination he pictured the farmers, the ranchmen, the miners, the people in the little towns, all bound together by the telephone, able to talk with one another.

"Hello," cried Woodrow Wilson into the black rubber tube. "Hello! I greet the great state of California from Washington, D.C.!"

But the President and the governor were not the only ones to take part in the demonstration of the telephone that day. For in New York, Alexander Graham Bell, white-bearded now, sat at a desk with another telephone before him, and in California, more than three thousand miles away, Thomas Watson was listening.

"Ahoy! Ahoy! Watson. Are you there? Do you hear me?"

"Perfectly," Watson answered. "I can hear every word."

Then there was a long pause while models of the old sending and receiving instruments were attached. They were exactly like the ones that Bell and Watson had used in the attic in Exeter Place thirty-nine years before. The new instruments were no better than the old ones, Bell maintained; the principle was the same. Now they were to be put to the test again.

At last everything was ready. Watson, the old receiver at his ear, sat waiting. Bell, his eyes brighter than usual, his cheeks a little redder, put the transmitter to his lips.

People wondered what speech he had prepared for this great day on which the telephone which he had invented was to carry
his voice all the way from the Atlantic
Coast to the Pacific. They had asked him,
but he had not been willing to tell.

Now, his eyes sparkling, his voice clear
and resonant, he spoke into his old transmitter: "Mr. Watson," he called across the
continent, "come here. I want you."

About the Author

Katherine Shippen was born in Hoboken, New Jersey. After graduating from Bryn Mawr College, she became a history teacher and school director. In her fifties Miss Shippen turned her talents to writing books for young people. Among the dozens of titles to her credit are *New Found World*, *The Great Heritage*, *Lightfoot*, and *Andrew Carnegie and the Age of Steel* (a Landmark Book). She died in 1980.